Raven

Also by Alan Wall from Shearsman Books

Gilgamesh
Alexander Pope at Twickenham
Doctor Placebo

The Shearsman Chapbook Series, 2012

Seren Adams : *Small History*
Kit Fryatt : *Rain Down Can*
Mark Goodwin : *Layers of Un*
Alan Wall : *Raven*
Michael Zand : *The Wire & other poems*

hors de série
Shira Dentz : *Leaf Weather*

Raven

Alan Wall

Shearsman Books

First published in the United Kingdom in 2012 by
Shearsman Books
50 Westons Hill Drive
Emersons Green
Bristol
BS16 7DF

www.shearsman.com

ISBN 978-1-84861-246-4

Contents

Raven and Serpent

The raven noticed the serpent
slithering lithely up the tree's trunk.
A beautiful garden.
One contented couple.

Raven was astounded when serpent spoke.
Now where, he wondered, did the snake learn that?
Are there summer schools these days down there?
Distance learning for winter visitors
even those descended from an unendowed urethra?

Raven's eye shone
bright as a moon if not the sun
when serpent's word
wormed its way down Eve's ear
through her delicate intestines
into her untried womb.

Could I do that? raven asked.
He asked (it should be said) in silence.
Such harmonies as rule here
rule unvocalised.

Noticed for the first time
how tastily the eyes of Adam gleamed

back now from the fields at last
arms filled with red red roses
for the lovely lady.

Emblem

Raven has returned to emblem books.

Of all his second homes
emblem books and bestiaries hold his preference.

There he strolls
admires himself in mirrors of engravings
reads how he never feeds his young
until black feathered quills break through.
Meets unicorn and cockatrice
centaur narwhal and chimera
nods *en passant* to fellow corvids. Never too friendly.

Likes to read about his preference for eyeballs
either on the battlefield
or on Tower Bridge where traitors' heads
get spiked up weekly for his delectation.

And, should he leave the nearby Tower
our kingdom falls in weeks.
Made a home for himself in the word ravenous
despite a host of weeping etymologists forbidding it.
Pruk-pruk, he says to all that. Mr Corvus. Mr Corvax.
Sometimes, while travelling abroad,
he'll answer to Raben or Corbeau

or even Kangee, shape-shifting cousin
from across the seas.

Once long ago his passport said *hraefn*.
and once, when Mighty Corvid issued his command
he fed Elijah who'd been telling
dark truths to kings.
All written out with a black feathered quill
supplied by yours truly.

Wishes they didn't portray him so often
striding over snow
things being seldom black and white like that.

Copernican

Never once doubted that the world was round
while your flat-footed granddaddy Neanderthals
took care they didn't look over the edge of things
and fall.

The world designed to fit exactly in each eyeball
ours or yours.

Something we ponder frequently enough
while chewing.

Migration

For centuries we stared from cliffs
at the itching
heaving
terrible flesh of the sea.

Then moved inland
for good.

Festivities

Once a year come Christmas
distant relatives arrive to tell their tales.
Here's *garrulus gladarius*
flashing his boutique colours
and his bling.

Then *pica pica*, blue and black and white
as though to wake a dozing farmer.

For ourselves we like the sable:
stay funereal, darkly-suited.

Appropriate avian ushers from on high
saving our *pruk-pruks* till later
when the real festivities begin.

For the record

Not one of us (not one)
ever uttered the word Nevermore.

And a gift for mimicry
not unlike your own
would mean
we never would repeat it
over and over like that.

One black-feathered bird perched inside
the troubled head of Edgar Allan Poe
had taken to drink.

A Peaceable Kingdom

Our relative the jackdaw, a friend from the east
likes the roofs of your castles
the more antique the better.
For ourselves we prefer mountains.
Virtuous men love mountains
wise men the sea—so I have heard.
In which case we are virtuous
our monogamy as unrelenting
as our plumage.

As for diet
needs must when the devil drives.
Today so far one mouse one shrew
one nesting infant from a neighbour's copse
beetles grubs
locusts and moths.

Keeping our heads cocked
for any sound of distant battle.
But you have grown pacific of late
hoping perhaps to starve us out with kindness.

Operatic

Sometimes at night I dream
trees and skies are one
and a derelict camper van
in the field below
has a god growing wise inside it.
He swallows winds
the way his antique fathers did in Egypt once.
Now and then
borrows the voice of a nearby television aerial.
An occasional rat climbs inside him to pray.
His words intermittent, lucid, terrible.
Prepare my dark-eyed friends
a mighty feast, he says.
And remember Belshazzar.

Winds sometimes shake these trees
a shudder loud enough to get life started
like one of those choruses from Wagner
where one world or another is dying.

Evensong

Once we all gathered on your cathedral roof
to hear you sing of kings
kings and saviours
the journey down and the journey upwards
men with wings and luminous hair
who fly in bearing messages from heaven
for blind old prophets crooked in their inglenooks.

We thought it wonderful.
If ravens could cry believe me we'd have wept.
Pruk-pruk, we chorused from our separate gargoyles.
Pruk
Pruk
Pruk.

Mimicry

Looking at your first
Howard Hughes contraptions
made us *pruk* so merrily
we pecked one another's feathers in jest.
They'll never get up here with us.

Closer to the dinosaurs ourselves
but you with that motorised snap of a brain
still count the crocodile brother.

Then you did it.

For a day and a night this kingdom of ravens fell silent.
They're dropping their eggs from the sky
we said, which can only mean
death-line meridians roped round the earth
like so many nooses.
Whole cities in a single night.
Such big metal eggs you'd fashioned.

Crocodile like ourselves
only kills what he plans to eat.
We both lack ambition here, clearly.

Stealth bombers even borrow our plumage.

Of late we lost our appetite for anthropoid eyes
you having offered us so many.

Itinerary

Went to Ravenna one year
since our wings still flutter in its name.
Also tried Ravensbrück.
plus countless hills and hamlets
perched on the Yorkshire horizon
whose names acknowledge our black eyes
our claws, our sense of
the ultimate fitness of things.

You could navigate a zigzag
grand tour
mapped out entirely
from our species nomenclature.

Pruk says the Norseman
faced with sorrows of the weather
a daily sarcasm of winds
a wave's malevolence when mounted.
Pruk-pruk.
Often set to bleak
if haunting music
blown through a narwhal's tusk.
Such keening laments.

Vikings could never see
one of us ravens without promptly shooting.
Death thou shalt die, it would seem
by mere assassination of the shadow's emblem-man.

Ritual and Decorum

He wishes the nightingale would cut it out.
Blackbirds and robins are almost as bad.
The humming-bird's come-hitherish flutter
in a famous naturalist's hand
while cameras roll
makes him proud of his anthracite speech.

One song.
One note.
One colour.

As for variety
let seasons do our changing for us.

Only nested in this Tower
having mistook it for a small riverside mountain.
Utterly startled when you turned up down there
wearing such fancy plumage and waving your blades
preparing for the morning sacrifice.

Watched in silence
Anne Boleyn's head slice off.
Wondered if it might be coming our way
but regal decorum said no.

Four raw eggs every morning in the hall of the Mess.
The ritual that gets a day started.
If ever they're late
we push into the breakfast room of the yeomanry
to ask what's going on now in the world of men.

Whispering Gallery

We picked your words up
gleaning detritus
in this disused coalmine.
The decorations down here suit our mood.
Colliers' oaths and lamentations
ventriloquize our religion so precisely
a Davy Lamp stands on the altar of our cathedral
whose address I may never divulge
to any other species (particularly yours).
Its flame glows eternal.
Before that, as you may recall,
you'd use caged birds to test for coaldamp or methane.
Their ghosts fly round here still
tiny fluttering atoms in darkness
searching for the blackened hands
of kindly men who fed them once.

www.ingramcontent.com/pod-product-compliance
Lightning Source LLC
Chambersburg PA
CBHW021950040426
42448CB00008B/1329